The Queen
Who Saved
Herself

Written by
Fiona J. Purcell

Fiona J. Purcell

"Defying Fortune's Spite"

Illustrated by Justine Babcock

I dedicate this book to Dermot Clavering Purcell (the healer of broken hearts), Wren Harrington Purcell (the soul songbird), baby Liam Walseth Purcell (forever our angel) and to their steadfastly protective and caring father, Francis Jerome Purcell III. They are my tribe and prove that families work in all sorts of forms when there is mutual respect, love and tolerance.

FORWARD

Coping with the impact of any disease is difficult and often painful. Finding support from those who have shared similar experiences can be comforting.

When addiction touches the family system, it wraps itself around every member, young and old, having an impact that can change how members understand and relate to one another. Children often suffer emotional and physical consequences of parental and sibling addiction. This can manifest itself in silence or acting out.

We know that families who receive a combination of education and support have positive outcomes. This is critical for each member of the family but especially for children who often feel isolated and bewildered about what is happening to their parent or sibling.

Author, Fiona Purcell, uses the story of "The Queen Who Saved Herself" as a reflection of a journey often traveled by a parent suffering from addiction and their child's experience. This story helps children understand that they are not alone and opens the door for a parent to have a healthy discussion with their child about addiction.

Hope leads the way and the Queen and her children find recovery that restores them.

Cheryl D. Knepper, MA, LPC, ATR-BC, CSAT-S, CMAT
VP, Caron Continuum of Care
Caron Treatment Centers

Once there was a young girl who grew up in a dark place.

She made it through the sad days of her childhood and emerged as
a young lady into a brighter world. She met a prince whom she thought
was charming. The Prince was excited to show her so many things!

They took time getting to know each other
and he grew protective of her. She felt
safe with him and they fell in love.

Eventually the couple married and they became King and Queen.

The young Queen thought being in love would solve all her problems and set her free from her dark, sad past. They had a Prince and then a baby Princess. These children opened the Queen's heart and showed her she was good inside. The little Prince was joy personified, and the Princess was like a song to their souls.

The King and Queen and the Prince and Princess lived in wonderful castles in many cities, moving each time the Queen became sad or restless. Even though she was surrounded by love and had all she ever wanted or needed, the King was unable to make her happy.
He was beside himself.

The King became sad and the Prince and Princess were scared.
No one knew what was wrong with the Queen. She had her King.
She had her Prince and her Princess and she had her wonderful castle.
She also had the King's family and many ladies-in-waiting.

Love surrounded her on all sides — what could possibly be wrong?

It turned out the Queen was haunted by dragons!

There was a black dragon from the dark days of her past
that was chained to her.
This dragon always hovered around
making her sad and feel bad about herself.

There was also a red dragon that spoke terrible things to her.

It would come and go but its voice was always loud. This dragon told her it could push away the black dragon, fix all her problems and make her feel good. But the red dragon lied! It made her act differently and do things she would never normally do. It led her to make bad decisions.

The Queen was afraid of the dragons and decided to tell the King about them. The King valiantly picked up a sword and tried to fight the dragons for her, but he could not see them to slay them.

It turned out the dragons were invisible to everyone but the Queen!

The King had to make a brave but heart-rending decision because he felt it was no longer safe for the Queen to watch over the young Prince and Princess. And so the Queen was sent away to take rest on a Magic Mountain. But the dragons followed her!

And she came to realize that no one but herself could slay them.

The Queen was distraught . . .
How would she manage to slay these
two dragons? She had never held a
sword . . . and she didn't
know if she was even
strong enough.

Once at the Magic Mountain, the Spirit of the Sky spoke to her and said, "Listen to ME — not the loud voice of the red dragon! I will guide you on a quest to rid yourself of both dragons and show you the road to happiness."

The Spirit then showed her to a path. He gave her a map and a list of twelve tasks.

The Queen would have to perform each task in turn as she made her way along the path. The Spirit of the Sky instructed her to seek help from an older, wiser queen who had gone down the path before her and who had completed all the tasks.

The Spirit encouraged the Queen and said he would always be there if she needed him.

But the Queen was afraid! She thought about how sad she was inside and knew she had to muster up the strength to go forth. She also thought of her brave King and of her young Prince and Princess and knew she could not return to them until she had rid herself of the dragons.

The twelve tasks seemed simple at first but they would require the Queen to be strong and brave.

And so her quest began!

Twelve Tasks

1: She would have to admit that she was powerless over the dragons and that her life was a mess.

2: She would have to start trusting in the Spirit of the Sky and the queens who had gone before her.

3: She would have to reach out and ask for help when she needed it.

4: She would have to make a list of all the mistakes she had made as well as all the things she liked about herself.

5: She would have to share her list with an older, wiser queen and the Spirit of the Sky.

6: She would have to decide if she was ready for the Spirit of the Sky to help her.

7. She would then have to ask the Spirit for help.

8. She would have to make a list of all the people she had hurt in her lifetime.

9. She would have to seek those people out and make things right with them.

10. Going forward from this point, when she made mistakes, she would have to make them right as soon as possible.

11. She would have to always remember to ask for help when it was needed.

12. Finally she would need to become an older, wiser queen herself and help other wandering queens on their quests for happiness.

The quest was long, and it was hard for the Queen. But with the help she had been given along the way she made it down the path, completed the tasks, and was finally strong enough to take up her sword. The Queen was able to fight off the red dragon and set the black dragon free!

The black dragon still hovers, but has moved further away.
It can't make her feel bad any longer.

The red dragon is wounded. It will
stay down as long as she remembers
not to listen to its terrible lies.

Now the Queen knows how to
fight her own battles!

The Queen thanked the Spirit of the Sky for showing her the path. Then the Spirit told the Queen the strength had been inside her all along — he had just shown her how to find it!

The King and Queen and the Prince and Princess could be happy again!

THANKS

It would be impossible for me to thank everyone who has helped me along my journey thus far, but I would like to thank a few people and institutions. My in-laws, Joan and Jerry Purcell, along with all the extended Purcell family, who have embraced me and have my best interests at heart; Caron Foundation for stabilizing me and starting me on the right path; Skip and Carole Mewhort and many others for providing invaluable guidance; Dr. William Heran and Gabe Lau for many new opportunities; my bridesmaids (ladies-in-waiting) Liz, Debbie, Mary Beth and Erin for always being there; Christine Estornell for her tireless work on the graphic design for this book. There are so many others including the backers of my Kickstarter campaign, and as for the rest, you know who you are and I am eternally grateful for all the love and support.

RESOURCES

If you or someone you know needs help with addiction, this list of twelve-step resources may help begin a journey of recovery.

Alcoholics Anonymous
www.aa.org
(212) 870-3400

Al-anon
www.al-anon.alateen.org (also the contact for alatot)
(757) 563-1600

Adult Children of Alcoholics
www.adultchildren.org
(310) 534-1815

Narcotics Anonymous
www.na.org
(818) 773-999

Nar-anon (for family and friends of someone with a drug addiction)
www.nar-anon.org
(310) 534-8188

Codependents Anonymous
www.coda.org
(602) 277-7991

The Queen Who Saved Herself · WORD SEARCH

Look up and down and diagonally to find the words listed below.

ADDICTION	FEELINGS	LIES	SAFE
ANXIOUS	FREEDOM	MAGIC	SECRETS
BATTLE	HAPPY	MIRACLE	SELF
BRAVE	HEAL	MOUNTAIN	SPIRIT
CONFUSED	HELP	PRINCE	STEPS
DISEASE	HOPE	PRINCESS	TWELVE
DRAGONS	INVISIBLE	PROBLEMS	
FAMILY	KING	QUEEN	

```
T F F X L L Z L O B D D U E K F U N L Q
Q P R O B L E M S I I N T Z Z L D G D F
H R Y S M O U N T A I N N S P D A T L A
L C S T E P S F H O P E A D E G L T A M
A I L K R P I R Z A N T U V H A H G N I
T W E L V E C C R U P T M L H L S D X L
X L L S Z S H E L P X P A U H E K E I Y
K Q C Q Y M C T P Y K S Y V J R Z I O L
A O P R I N C E Q V J I M Y Y U V B U V
W J Q M P R I N C E S S N D B Z L V S E
N R D R A G O N S L X J L G M R K K B I
S Y G E G K T H I F R P I Y A F A L S N
F R E E D O M T L M E E I U G P Z V O V
H H C W H B T B U S P E M R I Q Y O E I
E A L P M Z O U E E N Y L Q C A T F I S
L C F M C Y S A D D I C T I O N I S B I
Z Y Z C O N F U S E D L T L N R L A L B
R S P I R I T J R G A S E L F G V F Y L
M A M I R A C L E W F S H N D C S E X E
T S E C R E T S E H E A L B A T T L E V
```

Solution:

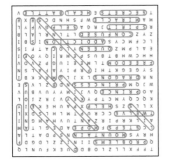

The Queen Who Saved Herself · **COLOR A DRAGON**

Can you see the Queen's dragons?
What colors will you make them?
Color them in!

The Queen Who Saved Herself • MAZE

After leaving her castle the Queen fought off dragons
and had to complete a list of twelve tasks.
But she had help along the way. Help her find the way to
the Magic Mountain and the Spirit of the Sky!

The Queen Who Saved Herself • **WORD SCRAMBLE**

Unscramble each set of letters below to make
a word related to recovery.
The first letter of each word is capitalized to get you started.

oochllA _____

elsmoPrb _____

eesaiDs _____

sgDnoar _____

eeRcvyro _____

reFemod _____

eisglenF _____

tpoSrpu _____

wordS _____

yiamFl _____

ltelBa _____

enlHiga _____

iseDase _____

evTwle _____

Aicdtd _____

rdiAaf _____

varBe _____

seSertc _____

Lvoe _____

inaP _____

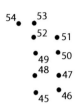

The Queen Who Saved Herself • CONNECT THE DOTS

The key to unlocking addiction can be found within yourself with the help of others. Connect the dots for the Queen!

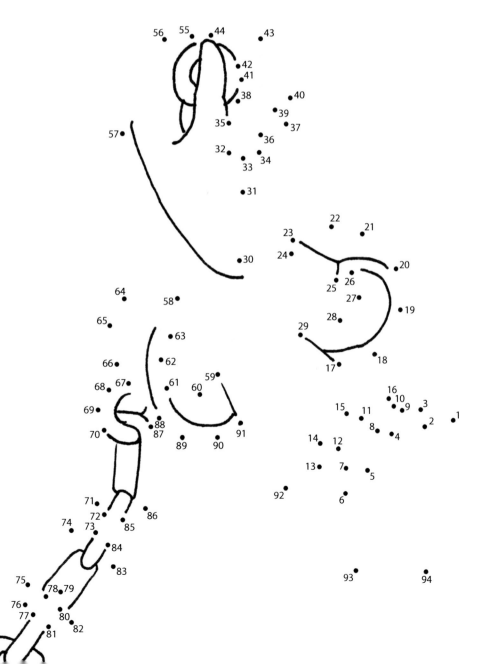

These next pages are for you!
After reading the story, describe or draw how you feel.
If someone in your life has been affected by addiction what
story can you tell about it?
Go ahead and draw what comes to mind!

Made in the USA
Middletown, DE
04 December 2017